Discover German Shepherds

by Victoria Marcos

xist Publishing

German Shepherds are working dogs.

They were first used to herd sheep.

4

They protect and herd many different animals. They want to have a purpose.

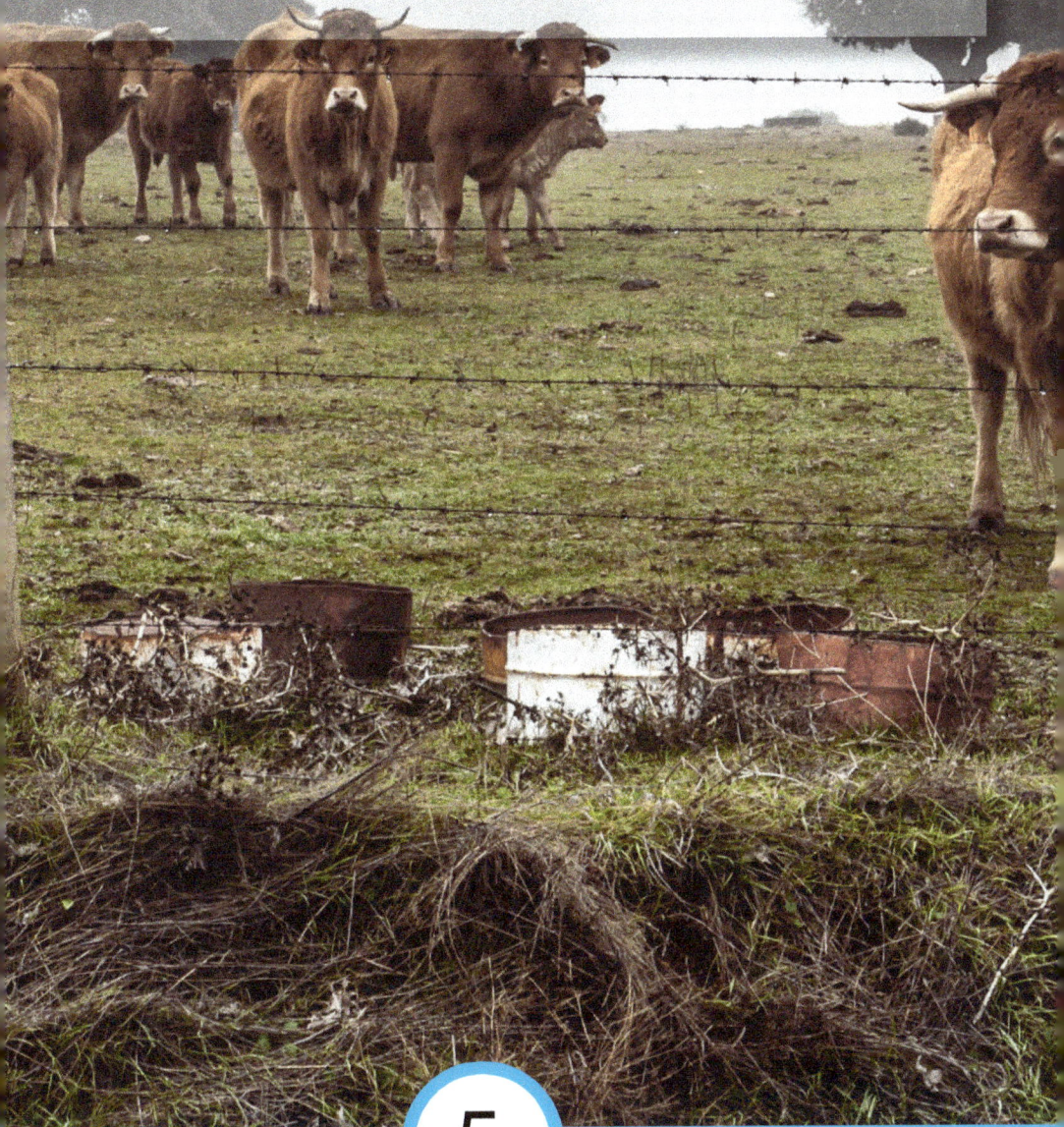

German Shepherds are very obedient and easy to train.

They are famous for their intelligence.

They learn tasks very quickly and obey correctly almost every time.

German Shepherds are used for search-and-rescue, police and military work.

11

They have an excellent sense of smell and aren't easily distracted from their work.

German Shepherds are also great swimmers.
They are very good at retrieving things from the water.

They are very active
and energetic.

Although German Shepherds are strong, they can also be very gentle.

There was a time when almost all Seeing Eye dogs were German Shepherds.

Well-trained
German Shepherds
are very safe.

They are very protective
of their families and territory.

They are especially
protective of children.

24

German Shepherds are great companions.

They are both gentle and trustworthy.

25

As puppies they need to be around many different people, sights and sounds.

They can live peacefully with other pets if they are taught as puppies.

Sometimes German Shepherds get sick. A veterinarian can help when they don't feel good.

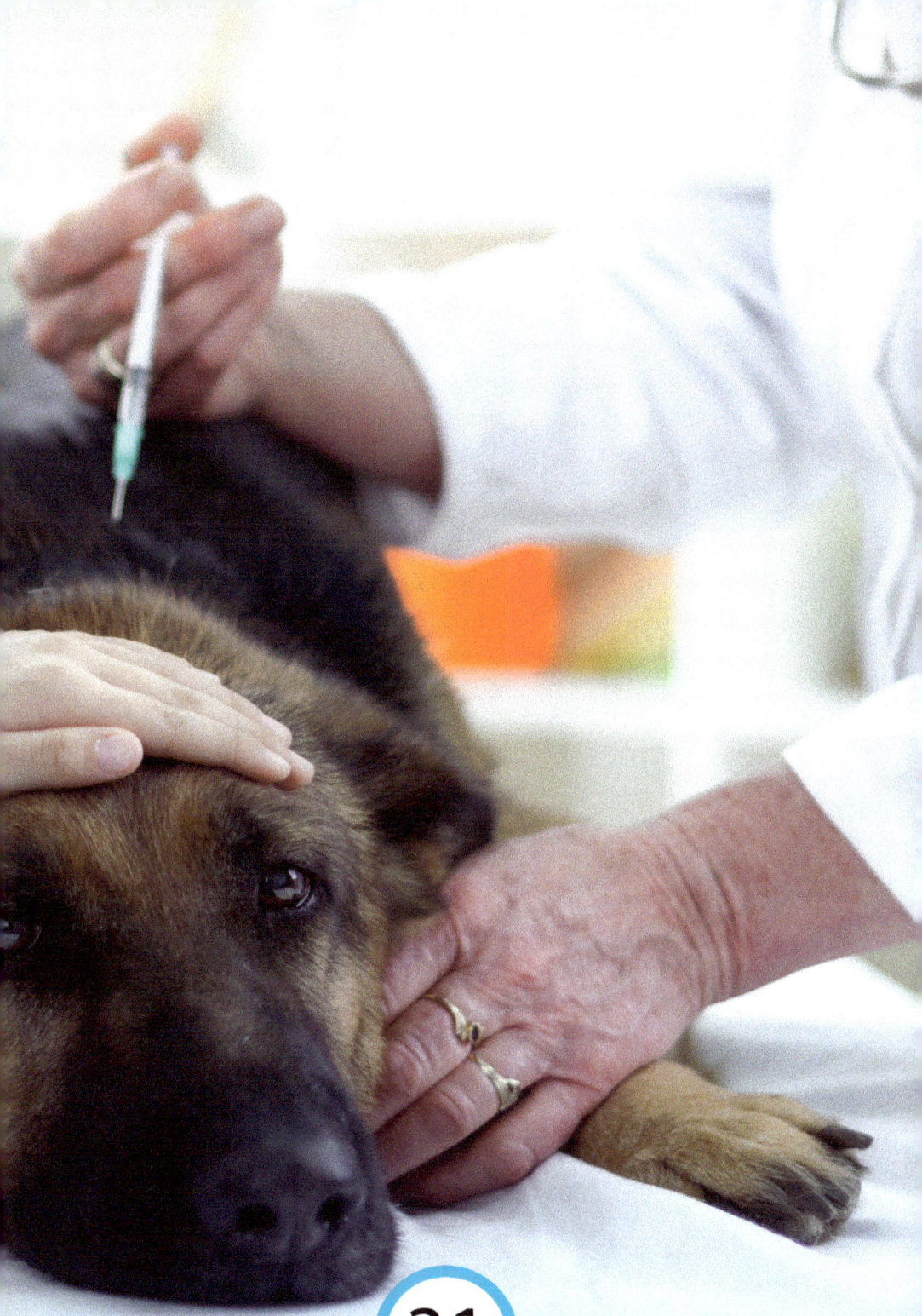

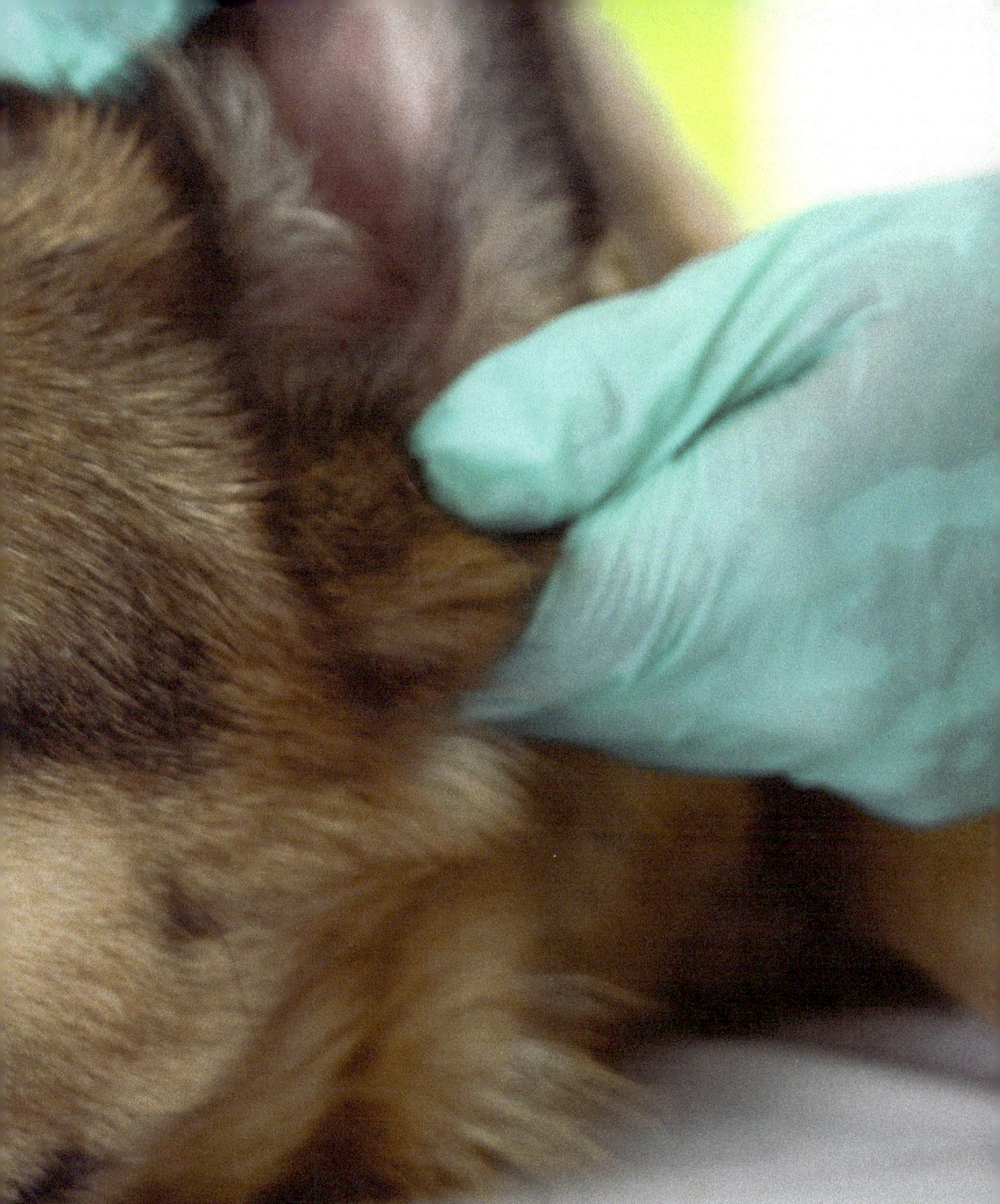

Some even get aches
like humans.

33

German Shepherds make for great friends.

www.ingramcontent.com/pod-product-compliance
Lightning Source LLC
Chambersburg PA
CBHW040417110426
42813CB00013B/2683